There is Hope—
Even If Your Brain Tells You There Isn't

Copyright © 2023 by Alicia White
Published by Chosen Stones Ministries
Email: Info@chosenstones.org
Web: www.ChosenStones.org

All illustrations and photos are copyrighted under Chosen Stones Ministries. Without written consent no illustrations or photos may be reproduced or copied for any reason.

Hope Noelle White

12/28/02 – 1/29/20

This is our "Hopie" as I affectionately call her. Hope, who loves to write, who loves to draw and paint, who loves the color yellow, sunflowers, and her dog, Revie, and her turtles, Squirt and Sheldon, is a forever beautiful 17-year-old.

Her hair is long and thick. Her eyes are a piercing deep brown. Her deep laugh is contagious, and her sense of humor is medicine for the soul. She can hit the lowest of notes and the highest of notes when she sings. She is beautiful inside and out, as a lover of Jesus and people.

This is our Hope: our daughter that we will never get to see, feel, hear, or even smell again on this side of heaven.

On January 29, 2020, Jesus received Hope home after her earthy battle with suicide. Hope loved Jesus and she loved people, but the battle for her mind was fought in silence, and the silence was Satan's weapon of choice to take her into hopelessness, and eventually it took her life here on earth.

Through Hope's story and her own personal journals, the power of Satan over a generation of youth and young adults who suffer in silence can and will be broken. Her story does not have to be yours. May you find the hope to live in Hope's story.

Most would not have imagined Hope ever battling with self-hate and low self-esteem in her mind. She hid it well behind many walls of protection. As her family, we knew about her struggle with self-esteem, but we had no idea just how badly she wrestled internally. Hope was very engaged in our church youth group. She was loved by so many and had numerous friends (more than she ever realized).

She had a genuine relationship with Jesus. Yes, she heard the voice of God. But as with us all, she also heard the voice of Satan. Satan preyed on her low self-esteem. He used everything he could to attack her weakness, like he does all of us. Due to her own insecurities, Hope often felt offended, hurt, and rejected. Because she felt unable to express those feelings, she often exploded at the littlest of things.

She began to believe that others thought about her the same way she thought of herself. This brought turmoil and tension in many of her friendships and family relationships, which only fueled more feelings of rejection and loneliness.

The day that changed our lives forever, January 29, 2020, was like any other day. We went to lunch together, laughed together, and had an argument in the car on the way home. A disagreement that was not much different than countless other arguments a mother would have with a daughter. Then thirty minutes later, she was gone. One moment, on one day, altered eternity forever.

Hope's struggle with low self-esteem is not unusual or rare. You may have already found similarities with your own story. Thousands of youth and young adults struggle in silence, and in the silence is where Satan is empowered. Hope's story lives in the eyes and hearts of countless people that feel shame and condemnation for feeling and thinking about such things as "self-harm" as believers of Jesus. Satan lies to us all. The mind is the true battlefield of any Christian. It is not the lie that defeated our Hope on this earth. It was her inability to cast down the lie and not allow it to become truth to her. Once the lie became her truth, it created a stronghold, shifting her reality and hijacking her decisions and her perspective on life. She kept this torment of the mind silent for anyone who could have helped.

There is Hope

You may feel alone and isolated in your own story and struggle. Satan may be silencing you in a cesspool of guilt, shame, and fear. But there is hope. Your story does not have to end like Hope's did.

After many months of grief, I finally had the courage to read her journals. What I found was hope, God's hope. She had journaled what Father God was speaking to her through words, drawings, and poems. He was speaking life into her very soul. God Himself was giving her reasons to live, she just failed to look beyond a moment in time and see herself as He saw her. I am certain the moment she did what she could not undo, she regretted it all.

As I read each page of her journals and looked upon the beautiful artwork and poems, I could hear Hope's voice, the Father's voice, speaking to a generation. Oh, how I have longed for Hope to walk back into the room, but what would she say if she did?

She would speak of hope: hope to live beyond a moment, a situation, a day, a year. If Hope walked into your very room this day, knowing what she knows now, she would share with you the words of your Father. She would tell you that your story does not have to end the way her story did.

This book is not a counseling book, a self-help book, or a cure-all for everything you're going through. If you are struggling with suicidal thoughts, you must reach out to

Christ-centered adults who can help you, especially your parents if you are a youth or young adult.

What I do believe is this: God's breath of life to you can be found within the pages of this little book. These are His words of hope, identity, and purpose. If you are struggling with heaviness, depression, low self-esteem, sadness, loneliness, purpose for living, the words of the Father penned by our sweet daughter Hope will bring life and truth to your mind and spirit. This book contains the seeds Hope left behind to be planted into a generation that needs to feel the Father's love and know they are not alone. This is a book of hope and the expected assurance of the goodness of the Lord.

May the seeds of Hope encourage you and help you find the hope of Jesus to live.

There is Hope

May 25th 2017

If your reading this, well I hope it helps you, or I hope that it will at least put a smile on your face. I just wanted to tell you how beautiful you are. I want you to know that if your reading this then you have helped me in my life tremendously. Let me tell you something your one of a kind. There is no one... Absolutely no one else like you. Yes beautiful you are so so so special. You might not feel like it right now but believe me you are. So many people care about you including me. Your not here by accident. You are going to do so much to change the world. You have a purpose and a destiny! In order to fulfill your purpose you must tell yourself, "No matter how hard it is, or how hard it gets, I'm going to make it." It does not matter what other people think or say. You never need to let other people's thoughts or actions control your life. Don't ever invest in things or people that don't invest back in you. Only invest in people that invest back in you. Many "things" will not go your way in life, But maybe seeing what will is the best adventure in life. Also remember you past does not define you. You can start the next chapter of your life if you always re-read the last one. You need to move on to bigger and better things. Your joy in life is one of the biggest things that matters in life. Please breathe and look at the positives in life. Happiness CAN be found even in the darkest of times, even when no-one is around. So beautiful remember your worth it and you so so so special. Don't forget to smile! So many people care about you!

Hope's Journal Entry
"Letter To My Friends"

There is Hope

Hope's letter reads:

If you are reading this, well I hope it helps you, or I hope that it will at least put a smile on your face. I just wanted to tell you how beautiful you are. I want you to know that if you are reading this then you have helped me in my life tremendously. Let me tell you something, you are one of a kind. There is no one... absolute no one else like you. Yes, beautiful, you are so so special. You might not feel like it right now but believe me you are. So many people care about you including me. You're not here by accident. You are going to do so much to change the world. You have a purpose and a destiny. In order to fulfill your purpose, you must tell yourself, "No matter how hard it is, or how hard it gets, I'm going to make it." It does not matter what other people think or say. You never need to let other people's thoughts or actions control your life. Do not ever invest in things or people that don't invest back in you. Only invest in people that invest back in you. Many things will not go your way in life, but maybe seeing what will, is the best adventure in life. Also remember your past does not define you. You cannot start the next chapter of your life if you always relive the last one. You need to move on to bigger and important things. Your joy in life is one of the biggest things that matters in life. Happiness CAN be found even in the darkest times, even when no one is around. So, beautiful, you're worth it and you're so so so special. Do not forget to smile! So many people care about you!!!

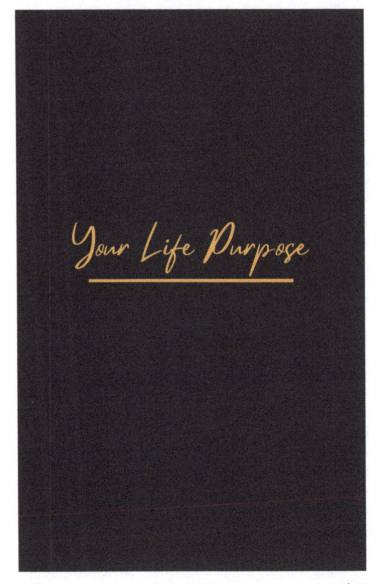

There is Hope

This letter she wrote was to her friends she knew, but I am certain that if she could, she would share it now with you and her entire generation.

With all my heart I believe this letter was from the Father, written to Hope, and as she journaled, she thought about her own friends who also needed to hear these words. I am amazed with the selfless way she encouraged others, but yet it was so hard for her to receive encouragement herself. Receive this letter of hope from Hope, and the Father today.

The day of Hope's funeral over 1500 people came to honor her. The church was filled with hundreds of peers, friends, people who loved her, and those who were touched by her life. After two hours, we still had not greeted everyone who had come. I remember looking out among the sea of people and thinking to myself what a tragic lie Hope had believed. She was loved; and loved by so many more than she ever realized.

Many of her friends struggled in school after her death. Some had to take a break from college. Others could not sleep alone in their bedrooms for months. Many had to go to counseling just to deal with the aftermath of loving someone who chose to take her own life. The damage and ripple effects of suicide go far beyond even immediate family.

The tragedy of death was not Hope's eternity. She knew Jesus, and she is beholding His glory even as you read this.

No, the tragedy is that Satan got her to believe a lie that eventually aborted her destiny and calling. God had a plan for her which He created before she was even conceived.

The joy her life was to bring to herself and others was cut short. The life experiences that the Father took good pleasure to plan for her were never fully realized. Yes, she would no doubt have experienced tough and hard things, but also things full of His perfect love and joy: her high school graduation, the trip to Colorado she had planned for her graduation vacation, meeting the man the Father had willed to be her helpmate, her wedding, having children. All these beautiful things that were unfulfilled in a life cut too short.

There is an even greater loss. The greatest tragedy of Hope taking her life was the eternity of others that may hang in the balance. The Father had an orchestra of people, places, and events that was to intersect with Hope's beautiful light, gifts, and love. These all were to come together with Jesus for lives to be changed, saved, and delivered. The Father needed her on this earth to make a difference in another person's soul. A husband was awaiting her and a whole new generation of children and their children. They were expecting her touch, planned by the Father Himself. Hope's unique fingerprint was left on the hearts of so many, but so many others will never feel and experience that touch. It is that altered destiny, and possibly eternity, of those left untouched by her life, that is the biggest tragedy.

I firmly believe the Father has plans for you that go far beyond your life and even your own eternity. And guess what? Satan knows that. If he can't keep you from eternity, he will try to get you to abort your own earthy destiny so others' eternities will be aborted.

Your life has purpose and meaning. You have something to do on this earth that no one else can accomplish. We don't all get an Olympic gold medal or become CEO of a fortune five hundred company, but we all have been born to love and make a deposit of goodness on this earth.

Read her letter over and over again and hear the Father's voice speaking to you. Say to yourself, "I'm going to make it." Keep saying it as many times as you need.

Hope's last Bible App picture posted just ten days before she passed

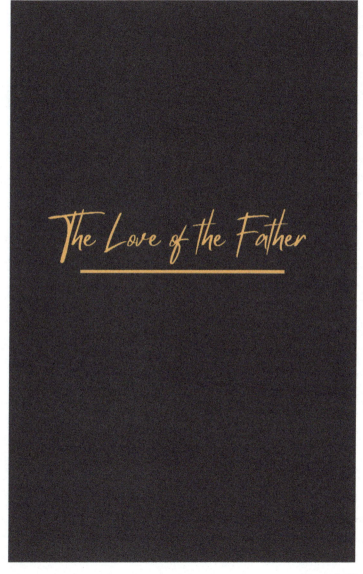

There is Hope

I have often thought about what would happen if Hope walked back into my room. If I could see her just one more time. What would I say? The only thing that would matter would be to say these three words to her, "I love you."

Love is the reason we live, breath, and get up each day. At the foundation of who we were created to be, is the need to be loved, and to love. Because of this, love is the very thing Satan tries to get us to believe we don't have. Love produces life, and without any love there is only hopelessness.

Many weeks after her death I had the courage to look at her entries on her Bible App. To my shocking surprise this picture "You are So Loved" was her last entry. Just ten days before her passing. Father God was speaking to her, and now He is speaking to you.

You might be asking, "So, if she believed she was so loved why did she take her own life?" What we know as truth and choose to feel in a moment are two different things. Sometimes our bad situation, our moment of fear and anxiety, our minute of anger and betrayal, smothers our ability to see truth. Our emotions often deceive our reality. The great tragedy is allowing one second of what we feel to change our lives forever.

If you are feeling unloved right now, or as if your life doesn't matter, I want you to know that is not truth. Beyond what I would say to Hope if she walked into the room, is what she would say to you and me. If she could come back from heaven, knowing all truth now, what would she say to you and me?

YOU ARE SO LOVED

If Hope could walk into your room, above all else, she would want to invite you to know the love of your heavenly Father.

"Can anything ever separate us from Christ's love? Does it mean he no longer loves us if we have trouble or calamity, or are persecuted, or hungry, or destitute, or in danger, or threatened with death? As the Scriptures say, "For your sake we are killed every day; we are being slaughtered like sheep. No, despite all these things, overwhelming victory is ours through Christ, who loved us.

And I am convinced that nothing can ever separate us from God's love. Neither death nor life, neither angels nor demons, neither our fears for today nor our worries about tomorrow—not even the powers of hell can separate us from God's love. No power in the sky above or in the earth below—indeed, nothing in all creation will ever be able to separate us from the love of God that is revealed in Christ Jesus our Lord." (Romans 8:31-39, NLT)

There is nothing you can do or not do that can make the Father not love you. He created you as His child, you were made in His image.

2 Corinthians 6:18 says, "I will be a Father to you, and you shall be My sons and daughters, says the LORD Almighty."

When you look in a mirror you may see your natural mother or father's eyes, hair, lips. You may even see what you don't like, but the Father sees Himself (Geneses 1:26-28). In the beginning in the Garden of Eden, the Father and His son Jesus desired a family. God chooses you to be His family. At first in the garden, it was perfect. Father God walked with His children, talking with them daily. When sin entered humanity, us, humanity chose to deny the love of the Father. Now, sin separates us from our Father in heaven, but God made a way. He made a way so all of His children could be with Him again. He sent His son, Jesus, who was and is just as perfect as His Father, to pay the ultimate price for our sin. He died so we didn't have to. As we receive Jesus as our savior, the Holy Spirit enters our spirit, and we become His sons and daughters. As a son or daughter of your heavenly Father, you are promised eternal life. You will have trials on this earth. We also die in our flesh, but you will live on in victory in eternal life. The good news of Jesus is about living eternally and living victoriously on the earth. He desires to give you His power to destroy the works of Satan in your life and live fully in your purpose here and now. His love is your power!

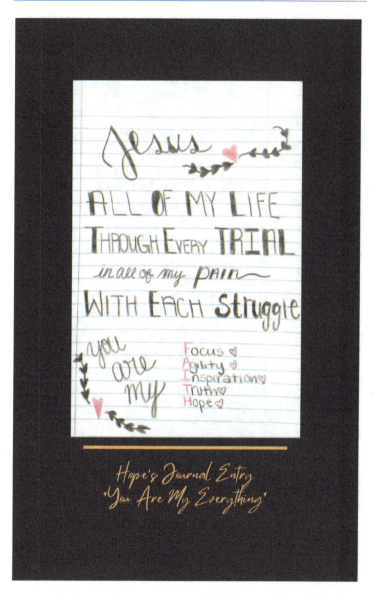

The power of the Father, through the Holy Spirit, brought Jesus back to life again. This resurrection power will defend you, fight for you, and give you victory throughout your life. If you will stay with your Father, receive His love, and follow His will for your life, He will become all you need.

I want you to understand today that no matter what life brings you or no matter what you decide to do in life, you are a son/daughter of Father God. He is not like any other father or mother. Your natural parents cannot always be there for you. We would like to think that every moment of every day when our child needs help, we can be there, but it just isn't going to happen. Whether you are at school, a friend's house, or alone in your bed at night, you will have times that you feel alone. You are never alone. Your heavenly Father is always present in your life. He will never die, and he will never leave you. Your natural parents will never be perfect. Parents mess up, and we mess up a lot! Your heavenly Father always gets it right. He is perfect in all His ways (Deuteronomy 32:4). He will never lead you on a wrong path or mistreat you. He will never hurt you, disappoint you, or misunderstand you. His love for you is perfect. People can only love with an imperfect love, but the Father loves you perfectly.

Your natural parents have limits. Your mom and dad are human, just like you. I can't tell you the amount of regret and "should have and would have" feelings I have had to battle since our Hope's passing. I didn't see things I should have seen. I didn't speak things I wish I had spoken. The love of any godly parent is deep, unconditional, eternal, but it is not perfect. The only one who is perfect, is your Father God. He desires to be ***everything*** to you.

Hope's Journal Entry
"My Help Comes From the Lord"

If you have not accepted His invitation today to come to Him, to become a son/daughter, now is a good time. I can't promise that life will be easy. Our Hope had accepted His invitation and still found herself in a place of struggle. This is where your journey of healing, joy, and abundant life starts. Your help and healing begin here. Jesus will help you from this day forward to walk through every situation if you let Him.

Accepting the Invitation Prayer:

Jesus I am broken. I need you. I believe you created me to be your child and I accept that invitation right now. I believe you took my place on the cross so I could live and not die, and with you I can face each moment and situation. Come into my very spirit and live and breathe in me. Save me.

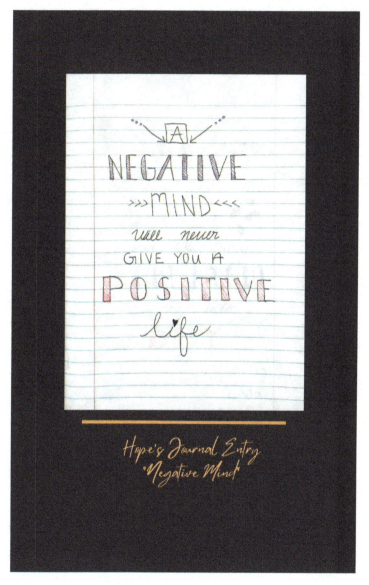

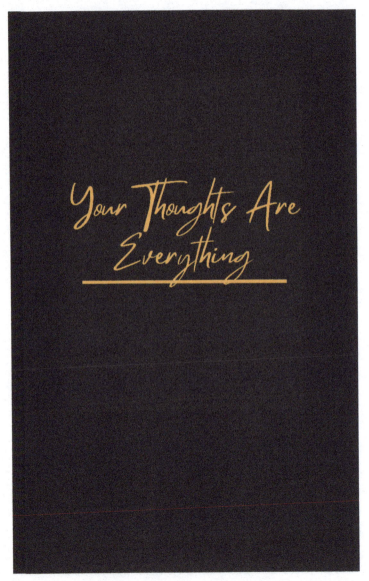

Philippians 4:8 says, "Finally, brethren, whatever things are true, whatever things are noble, whatever things are just, whatever things are pure, whatever things are lovely, whatever things are of good report, if there is any virtue and if there is anything praiseworthy— meditate on these things."

Listen to me carefully. Everything you will ever do in life will begin with a thought. One entertained thought can literally shift your whole entire life in one moment. This was where it went wrong for Hope, but it doesn't have to go wrong for you. Every thought requires a response. One way or another we respond. We either entertain the thought until it becomes our truth, or we cast it down and do not allow it to take root.

"Casting down arguments and every high thing that exalts itself against the knowledge of God, bringing every thought into captivity to the obedience of Christ." (2 Corinthians 10:5)

Negative thoughts will come. They come to us all. It is what you do with them that matters.

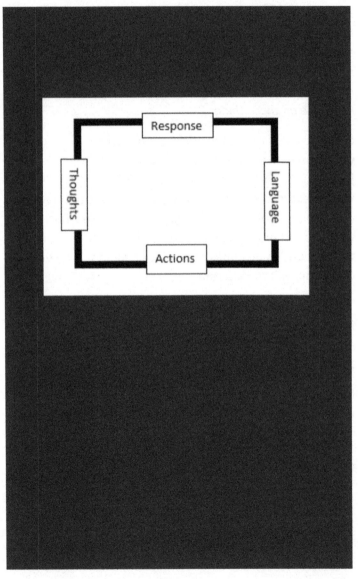

There is Hope

We are all framed up by our thoughts. Just like every good picture is displayed in a frame, so are we. In a generation of selfies and social media, images are extremely powerful. Whether you know it or not, your image is framed up in, or held together by, whatever you think. Those thoughts, whether good or bad, determine your actions.

If you rely on the world and culture around you to tell you who you are, your frame (what holds you up) will become what others say you are. People are imperfect, conditional, and ever changing. Your frame will become weak, full of lies and manipulation. If your thoughts are fed by the Father's words, love, truth, and plans for you, your frame, (what holds you together) will be determined by the vast, deep, wide, endless love of the Father. Your frame will become strong enough to hold you up in the trials and storms of life.

Here is how your frame works: every entertained and accepted thought will begin to alter and shift your language. Your language is a very powerful thing. God used language to create every living thing and all of creation. He made you in His image and you must know He has given you the power of life and death in your tongue (Proverbs 8:21). Rooted thoughts, thoughts that becomes truth to you, will shift your language. You may try to control your tongue around some, but you will not be able to escape the effect that a thought you have received as truth will have on what you speak. Next, comes the final stage of all thoughts: your actions. The decisions you make in life are based upon your language, which is based upon your response, which is based upon an entertained thought that has become truth to you. This is your frame.

Once you have become a son/daughter of God, Satan cannot enter your spirit. The only place he has access to try to destroy you, is your thought life. No one is exempt from his attacks in this area. He began to get Hope to believe she was not good enough, pretty enough, smart enough, loved enough, that she had no friends, and on and on. Satan preyed on her low self-esteem, and her lack of understanding of her identity in Christ and Hope lost sight of the truth that she was made in the Father's image and a daughter of the most-high God. She believed that everyone thought of her the same way she thought of herself.

This may even be true for you today, but you have the power within you to shift what you are thinking. Your frame begins with your thought life. Ask the Holy Spirit to help you today, and to show you when you are straying from His truth and His thoughts. It takes effort and work to keep our minds on the right things, but the power of the Holy Spirit can and will help you. You also need adult believers, and maybe a Christian counselor, that you can confide in to help you with your thought life. The first person we should always turn to is Jesus, but you will need help from other mature believers, pastors, leaders, and even counselors if your thoughts are affecting your frame of life.

There is Hope

Hope's Painting
"The Garden"

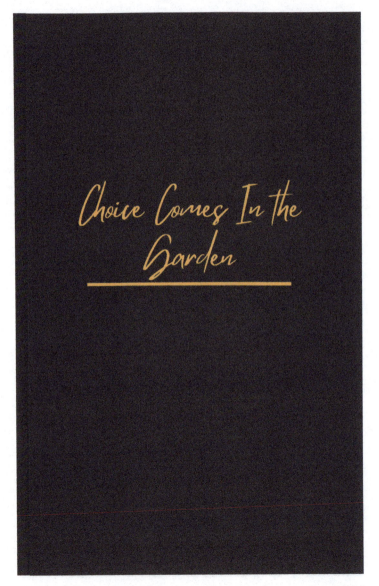

There is Hope

Done　　　　　　　　**Moment**

Hope White highlighted Genesis 3:2-7 NIV

² The woman said to the serpent, "We may eat fruit from the trees in the garden, ³ but God did say, 'You must not eat fruit from the tree that is in the middle of the garden, and you must not touch it, or you will die.' " ⁴ "You will not certainly die," the serpent said to the woman. ⁵ "For God knows that when you eat from it your eyes will be opened, and you will be like God, knowing good and evil." ⁶ When the woman saw that the fruit of the tree was good for food and pleasing to the eye, and also desirable for gaining wisdom, she took some and ate it. She also gave some to her husband, who was with her, and he ate it. ⁷ Then the eyes of both of them were opened, and they realized they were naked; so they sewed fig leaves together and made coverings for themselves.

Hope's Last Bible App Entry

There is Hope

This was Hope's last scripture highlighted in her Bible app: just one week before her passing. The words that Satan spoke to Eve in that garden, one way or another, are the words he speaks to us all. Satan desired to get Eve to believe the lie that she was not good enough, pretty enough, loved enough, smart enough, the way she was created. He got her to forget who she was, a daughter of God almighty. He manipulated her to devalue herself to the point that she killed herself. Yes, Eve and Adam, committed suicide. Not in the way we typically think of it, but it was both a spiritual and physical suicide.

All of humanity was promised to live forever until the choice was made to believe the lie of Satan and eat of the forbidden fruit of good and evil. That choice brought death, not just to Adam and Eve, but to all of humanity. It also separated them from their Father and caused us all to live in sin, in need of our savior, Jesus.

We all have garden moments where we are faced with a choice. A choice of thought; a choice of what we are going to believe as truth. Like Eve, it is possible to have a relationship with God, talk with Him and walk with Him, yet allow one moment, one emotion, one thought to overcome the truth you know. Hope no doubt had that moment, maybe even moments, and chose temporarily to believe a lie that led to a permanent decision. A mirror of Eve in the garden.

Jesus had a similar moment in the garden as well. Actually, He had three "garden moments" that we know of, except one wasn't in a physical setting of a garden, but in a desert. Satan came to Jesus, the son of the living God, and entered His thoughts. He twisted all kinds of scripture to try to change the thought life of Jesus. Remember it all starts with a thought. However, Jesus, who is perfect in all ways, made the choice not to believe the thoughts of Satan. He spoke the word of God to Satan instead. He knew who He was and His identity in the Father, His "frame," kept him from falling into temptation. You can read this entire story in Matthew 4:1-11.

The second garden moment for Jesus was in the Garden of Gethsemane where he was emotionally and physically overcome with weakness and sorrow, to the point of death, scripture tells us. The sin of all of humanity was being placed upon Him, preparing Him to die a sacrificial death for our lives. The pain, grief, and sorrow were almost too much. Scripture said he sweated great drops of blood from the emotional agony of sin and pain. He asked His Father in a moment of weakness to allow Him to not suffer what He was called to do. What He was feeling in one moment of time was so overwhelming that He almost walked away from His entire calling on this earth. Have you been there? Are you there now?

As He prayed to the Father His response became, *"Not My will but Yours be done,"* Luke 22:44 (NKJV). Jesus even set the example in that moment and asked his closest disciples (friends) to pray for Him as well. Although they failed miserably, Jesus demonstrated to us that we need each other. Get some good solid prayer partners to intercede for you in your garden moment.

Praying to the Father and surrendering to His will and ways in our lives, is key to keeping up our strength and ability to resist temptation. Holy surrender to the Father, whom you can trust to keep and strengthen you, will get you through anything you face in life. He has not called you with a purpose to let you fail, unable to accomplish it. Although, it may seem that way sometimes, just like it did for Jesus, choose the Father's will for your life. Let Him strengthen you. You can read the entire story in Luke 22:39-4.

The third garden moment for Jesus was at His tomb. After Jesus fought the battles of the garden and surrendered to the will of His Father, He fulfilled His ultimate calling and purpose on this earth by dying a sacrificial death on the cross for all of humanity. He died on the cross, so you did not have to. Here is the third garden moment. Mary came to Jesus' tomb and the stone was rolled away. Jesus had risen from the dead. Just like Jesus, if you stand and defeat temptation in your life through the Word of God, prayer, and surrender, you will see the resurrection power of Jesus. You will wake to a new day, a new season, and feel life again. Read Mark 16.

There is Hope

Hope's Drawing
"Awake a Generation"

Our garden moments, and the fruit of the tree of life and death that's on it, come in many forms. For some they may be drugs, alcohol, pornography, and other addictions. For some they might be acts of violence. Others may experience depression or suicidal thoughts. Today one of the biggest garden moments goes unnoticed because it is so ingrained into our culture: social media.

Social media can be a fruit from Satan's tree. It was for Hope, and it could be for you too. You look at one picture in which you were not included, one post of what a friend did, a photoshopped perfect image that you can never be, 3 likes to their 100 likes, and without one word spoken thoughts of insignificance flood your head. There is a documentary out called **Social Dilemma**. Many of the top players that helped invent and distribute social media were interviewed. They told stories of how much control "Big Tech" has over your thoughts and actions. The suicide rate for kids and youth since social media became available on our phones has more than doubled. I am not saying you should not use social media, I use it, but it is very important that you are aware of how it affects your thoughts and emotions. If you often feel rejected, angry, lonely, or sad after scrolling or posting, it is important for you to take a break from it. You need to learn how to deal with your emotions in a healthier way.

This world is controlled by Satan, who would like nothing more than for you to be led by your emotions. Our emotions are a gift from God, but they should always be

There is Hope

subject to the truth of God's word and the Spirit of the Father within us. Be wise and aware of how Satan is trying to manipulate your mind. We do not wrestle against flesh and blood. People are not your enemy. Satan is and him alone.

Often when we are struggling with Satan's fruit, he makes us feel ashamed and tries to silence our cry for help. I find this especially true for believers. We feel like people will question if we truly love Jesus if we are battling such things in our lives. But silence is Satan's weapon of power. The more he can keep you ashamed and silent, the more power and control he gains in your life. We had no idea of Hope's struggle with suicidal thoughts. If we had, I can promise you I would not have made her feel bad. I would not have shamed her or been disappointed in her. I would have gotten her the help she needed to take control of her thoughts. It is important for you to speak up and share with someone who can counsel you.

The first person we should always turn to with our struggles is Jesus. He can do what we cannot do ourselves. You will also need help from other mature believers, pastors, leaders, and even counselors if you are struggling with thoughts, addictions, or situations that could potentially harm you or others.

Sharing with someone who can help is key. Often when we struggle with something, we feel ashamed or embarrassed. Our first instinct is to tell someone who we think will understand, such as a friend or peer that struggles with the same thing. This can sometimes do more harm than good. You may find comfort with your peers, but if they are not adults that know how to support you, or they themselves struggle with the same issue, you will never truly find help. Misery loves company, and Satan loves that company. An alcoholic in the throes of addiction will never be able to help another alcoholic free himself. This is true for any fruit of Satan with which we struggle.

Don't believe the lie of Satan and find comradery but not the help you need. In the back of this book, I have listed suggested resources for assistance and support. If your parents are following Jesus, first go to them. If they are not following Jesus, get connected with a church and reach out to a pastor or Christian counselor.

There is Hope

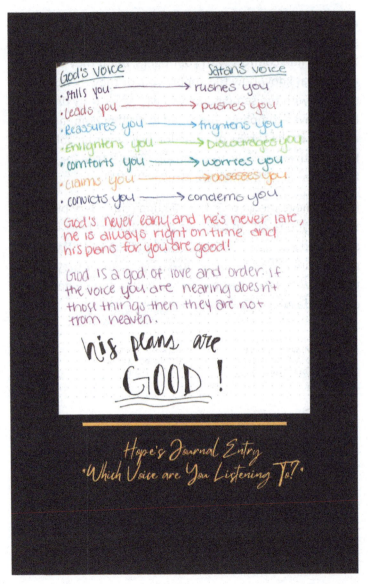

Hope's Journal Entry
"Which Voice are You Listening To?"

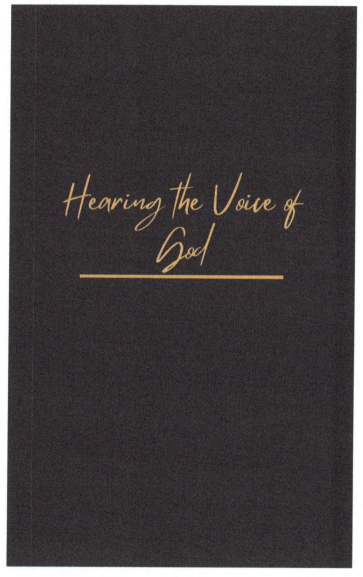

Hearing the Voice of God

If you have accepted the invitation to be a son/daughter of your heavenly Father, He desires to speak to you. In fact, He IS speaking to you, but you may not recognize His voice above all the noise around you. Hope's journal entry on the differences between God's voice and Satan's voice is very powerful. It is important that you stop and meditate on the thoughts with which you are struggling. If those thoughts bring negative emotions, they are most likely not from God.

The Father too has thoughts He wants to give you. He wants you to see in yourself greatness, beauty and courage. Also, He gives you the power to cast down every thought not from Him and receive His truth about who you really are. You are not a disappointment, you are not a mistake, and you are not a screw-up. You are made in the very image of your Father. You have His DNA, His blood runs through your veins, and you are His cherished gift. He is not mad at you, but madly in love with you. Lou Engle said, "Sons and daughters of the Father are simply a dream of God wrapped up in flesh." Your life is bigger than you or even the people you know and love right now. You are part of something bigger than yourself. The Father desires that you see past one moment in time, to see the bigger picture of the joy set before you. Yes Joy! You may not feel joy right now, see it, or have any hope for it, but the One who created you does.

There is Hope

"For I know the plans I have for you," declares the Lord, "plans to prosper you and not to harm you, plans to give you hope and a future." (Jeremiah 29:11, NKJV)

This world is full of noise from our phones, computers, tablets, and gaming stations. We all live inside our bubble of social media, TikTok, YouTube, and whatever else the next trend will bring. Noise drowns out the silence, but often it is in the silence where you will hear the voice of God best. Not that He doesn't speak at other times, but we must be willing to tune our ears to Him and pay attention. Often His voice isn't heard audibly, but sometimes God speaks through an action. God speaks by using everyday situations. He loves to bring you sudden moments that makes you stop in your tracks, and without question, know He is speaking. You could be in the classroom, at work, hanging out with a friend and a "suddenly" moment may come out of nowhere. Be open to hearing His voice above the noise.

There is Hope

13 REASONS WHY NOT ....

1. you are loved (John 3:16)
2. you have a purpose (Jeremiah 29:11)
3. you are given strenth to perserve (1 Corinthians 10:13)
4. you will be guided (psalms 32:8)
5. you are not alone (deuteronomy 31:6)
6. you were created by him & for his glory (Isaiah 43:7)
7. He will take away your worries (1 peter 5:7)
8. He will comfort you (2 corinthians 1:3-4)
9. He will carry your burdens (psalms 55:22)
10. He will forgive (Mark 11:25)
11. He will give you hope (Romans 15:13)
12. He will deliver (Matthew 7:7)
13. He dwells in you (1 Corinthians 3:16-17)

you WILL be OKAY!

Hope's Journal Entry
"Thirteen Reasons Why Not to Kill Yourself"

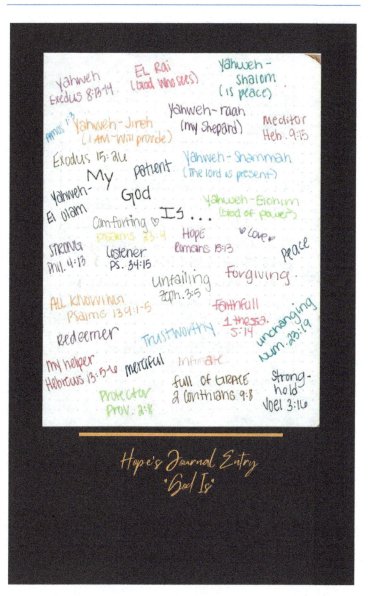

Hope's Journal Entry
"God Is"

He Doesn't Take Control

There is Hope

These two journal entries written side by side each other are the only evidence we have that Hope struggled with suicidal thoughts. Actually, the journal passages hold incredible truths that refute the thoughts she was having in her mind. Her written words gave so many reasons for choosing life instead of death.

So, you might be thinking, "If Hope journaled these things, why did she still choose to end her life?" "If it didn't help her, why would it help me?" That is a complicated answer with a lot of different reasons behind it, some of which we have already talked about.

For a minute, let's talk about choice. I am confident that if Hope had opened up her own journal on January 29th and read the words of the Father, penned in her own handwriting, she would not have made the impulsive decision to end her life. If Hope, taken a deep breath, read what the Father thought of her and who He is, her breath would have become His. God's peace would have filled and overtaken her.

Instead, Hope chose to follow the trail to the fruit of Satan, and just like Eve, she took a bite. Satan's voice became the only voice she listened to that day. Her "frame," who she thought she was, became weak. Satan lied to Eve when he told her that she would not die after eating the fruit. I believe he fed this lie to Hope too. I think she wanted to cry out for help, but, like so many others, she felt silenced by the enemy. We don't believe Hope thought she would die that day. Tragically, she made the choice and Satan doesn't play fair. It's all about choices.

You might be asking, "If all those things Hope journaled are true about God, then how could He let her make that choice?"

Think about it for a moment…do you really want to serve a God who controls you like a robot or puppet? Would that make Him more loving? There is a partnership, and at times a war, between the perfect will of the Father and the sovereign law of humanity's choice. His perfect will was that Adam and Eve would not eat the fruit from the tree of the knowledge of Good and Evil, but He allowed them to do so. When Adam and Eve disobeyed God, sin, evil, and sickness entered the earth. There were consequences for their choices. Because of this, we also live with consequences.

God cannot go back on His own laws and principles for His kingdom and earth. So why does God allow evil and sin to hurt people? If he intervened and didn't allow our choices, He would be going against the laws of His own kingdom. God is not a man who would lie. His character is true and holy. He cannot rebel against creation's laws. To do so would mean to abort the heart of humanity. He would not have the pleasure of authentic relationship with His children. It would be forced, religious, and heartless. I recently heard Steven Furtick make this profound statement, "God is *always* in control, yet He does not always *take* control." The Father took His hands off the wheel with Adam and Eve, and He does at times with you and me. He refuses to take control of the heart and soul of His children with the greater hope that they would choose to follow Him.

God's perfect will for Hope, and for you, is to live and not die. He gave you life. Let Him choose when it is time to go from this life to eternity. He knows the plans He has for you and they are good. Choose life!

There is Hope

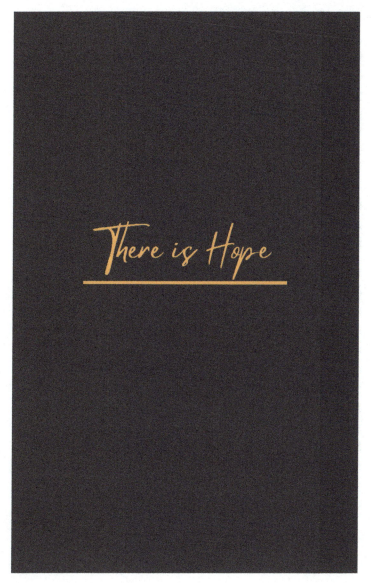

There is Hope

The love of the Father gives us choice, but His love also redeems us when those choices aren't what God would have wanted. When we make the wrong choices in life, when we mess up, sin, and get ourselves into trouble, the blood of Jesus is always there to forgive us and bring us back into right standing with Him...if we allow Him to.

All mistakes can be forgiven, but not all mistakes are easy to correct. If you go down the road of addiction, you can come back from that, but it is a choice to come back. God's power, love, and mercy will help free you from any enslavement, but you have to want to be free and willing to do the necessary work.

Suicide, however, is just about the only thing, if not *the* only thing, you can't correct. God's love is unconditional. His love for Hope has never gone away, nor His forgiveness. Because she was a child of God, the moment she chose to take her life, the Father forgave her. This is why I have assurance that she is now in heaven with Him. Our salvation is not based upon our perfection, but upon what Jesus did on the cross for us. Although I have hope I will see her again in heaven, I will never see her again on earth. Suicide, unlike other sins, is not reversable. This is why it is so important to understand that no matter what you are going through, you CAN make it! There is always hope. Choose to live!

There is Hope

Hope is the expectation that the goodness of the Father will come to you…even when your brain tells you otherwise.

Because of the death and resurrection of Jesus, we can always have hope. Satan speaks the opposite of what the truth really is. He told Eve she would not die, when in fact, death was exactly what happened. Satan cannot enter the spirit of man as long as Jesus resides there. His only chance of destroying you as a son or daughter, is to make his voice louder than Jesus' voice in your ear. He then deposits his lies in your brain.

This is what happened to Hope. Satan attacked Hope's thought life, bringing hopelessness to her brain. He attacked her very identity, for she was called to be Hope to the hopeless. God named her Hope for a reason, and He has named and called you for a reason and purpose too.

There is always a way of escape with Jesus. He defeated hopelessness at the cross; you just have to receive His free gift. His joy will become your strength and His perfect love will cast out all fear. You don't have to win, because Jesus won for you. All He expects of you is to trust Him, believe in His word, and keep moving forward. His mercy is new each day.

There have been days since Hope's passing that I felt like I could not go on, but another day did arrive. I found that when I was at my lowest, Jesus picked me up and carried me until the sun shined again into my heart. He will do the same for you.

There is always hope, even when your brain tells you there isn't!

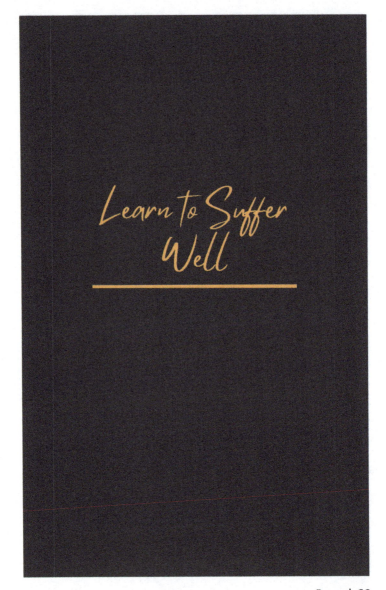

There is Hope

I felt led to share with you my own places of pain and suffering on my journey of losing my daughter, to help the younger generation learn how to "suffer well." Time has passed since our daughter's death, and I have realized the key thing determining the outcome of pain is how well someone learns to suffer in this world. When our daughter passed, we had two roads ahead. One would lead down a long, dark place of hopelessness and death. The other would lead us into hope, life, and strength to overcome the pain. Our daughter Hope experienced pain and suffering just like we all do. No one escapes hardships on this earth. Perhaps learning some key tools to overcome pain might shift the outcome for those who are suffering. It is my prayer that the truths that I have learned may help you find your way to overcoming things life throws at you.

I remember feeling the very raw painful place of suffering and loss from Hope's passing. I cried out in despair thinking that I had lost not only my daughter, but the faith I had in my Savior. But this was a lie from the enemy. Our Hope was not gone forever, she was very much alive and living, just not where we were. In addition, the hope of my Father had not left either. I could experience and obtain that hope by learning to "suffer well." Suffering well means not just surviving but learning to thrive. It means to suffer in such a way that you become better, not bitter. In the midst of pain, you learn to find life, joy, and even purpose. You become an overcomer by learning to walk out your pain with the one who overcame it all for you - Jesus.

In John 16:33 Jesus says, "I have told you all this so that you may have peace in me. Here on earth, you will have many trials and sorrows. But take heart, because I have overcome the world" (NLT). Jesus himself tells you that there will be pain and suffering in this world. Since the fall of man, we have had a constant battle with sin, sickness, and all kinds of destruction. But Jesus made a way for your victory through the cross. If you allow him to work in you, he will use every bit of the pain and suffering for your benefit. There will be extremely painful things in this life that you won't like and cannot change. Suffering does not discriminate. It happens to us all. Pain and sorrow could be within your home or in your relationships.

Goodness of the Father

Grief can occur at any time. Just as we can count on pain and suffering in this world, we can also count on the goodness of the Father. "I would have lost heart, unless I had believed that I would see the goodness of the LORD in the land of the living," (Psalms 27:13, NKJV). The Father's goodness in the place of pain is called hope. It is the anchor for your soul. It secures you to the rock, Jesus Christ. When the waves of pain and unchangeable circumstances come your way, he will provide his goodness. His goodness can be found in the darkest of nights. It is the joy of knowing that he will take away all pain and suffering and replace it with his goodness and mercy.

"Keep your eyes on Jesus, who both began and finished this race we're in. Study how he did it. Because he never lost sight of where he was headed—that exhilarating finish in and with God—he could put up with anything along the way: Cross, shame, whatever. And now he's there, in the place of honor, right alongside God. When you find yourselves flagging in your faith, go over that story again, item by item, that long litany of hostility he plowed through. That will shoot adrenaline into your souls!" (MSG). The joy set before Christ in the dark place of suffering was knowing the goodness of the Lord would prevail. Your pain and suffering will bring life and hope if you allow it.

Without hope, despair will drag you slowly into a very dark place surrounded by the lies of Satan and the spirit of death will suck out any joy within.

"And not only that, but we also glory in tribulations, knowing that tribulation produces perseverance; and perseverance, character; and character, hope. Now hope does not disappoint, because the love of God has been poured out in our hearts by the Holy Spirit who was given to us" (Romans 5:3-5, NKJV).

Learn to Take on the Character of Jesus

At the end of pain and suffering, there is always hope in Christ. This scripture tells us we must DO the will of the father in order to obtain hope. The character of Christ produces this hope. You must learn how to suffer well inside the character and nature of Christ. We must demonstrate his fruit in our lives no matter what has happened, how much you are hurting, or how unfair the circumstances. Keep your eyes on Jesus and do what pleases the Father. If our daughter had been able to do this, she would be alive today. Life is always found in Jesus. Satan will give you opportunities to look away and respond out of emotions and not truth. He will take you to a place that brings pain, addictions, ungodly behavior, and hurt towards others and yourself. Be in Christ and do what he would do, say what he would say, and think as he would think.

"Don't copy the behavior and customs of this world, but let God transform you into a new person by changing the way you think. Then you will learn to know God's will for you, which is good and pleasing and perfect" (Romans 12;2, NLT). Often painful circumstances lead us to question the will of God for our lives. We begin to think we don't deserve to be happy, and our circumstances will never change. But the Father's thoughts for us are for good and not destruction. If you allow it, suffering can create opportunities for growth and transformation. This is the very reason we are to live as followers of Christ. We want to be transformed into the likeness of Jesus, so his perfect will and goodness lead us in everything we think and do. Your perspective will determine your character. When pain comes our way we often only see through our own eyes. Jesus desires that we see all pain and suffering through his own. I had to do this when my daughter died. I had to seek the Father's perspective in order to survive the pain. Whatever you are going through, ask Jesus to show you his perspective. The Father is not the author of pain and suffering, but he will use it to transform your mind into the mind of Christ.

Learn to Forgive

When you begin to think like Jesus, you respond like him in your pain. This may look like forgiveness. We forgive those who have caused us pain because we know not forgiving will only bring more pain. Hope posted a phrase on social media before she passed that said, "Unforgiveness gives power of your life to the one who has hurt you." When walking with hate, anger, or resentment towards someone, that person has more power over your life than you have. Ephesians 4:32 says, "And be kind to one another, tenderhearted, forgiving one another, even as God in Christ forgave you." This is not always easy and sometimes may seem impossible. But if you suffer inside of Christ, he will give you the grace to forgive. Don't allow someone else to hold you back from being who you were called to be, a son or daughter of Christ. You were called to forgive as Jesus continues to do for each one of us. If you do this hard thing you will find your way to hope.

Sometimes that forgiveness may even have to be extended to yourself. This was one of my biggest battles. Forgiving myself after my daughter passed seemed impossible. Maybe you feel your situation is too awful to deserve forgiveness. The Father's grace reaches beyond anything you may have done. The work of the cross is for you. He sees you through eyes of love and this is how we are to see ourselves and others.

Learn to Face the Pain

Responding to suffering inside of the heart of Christ, often means embracing your place of pain. When pain hits, our response is to put on a tough shell and pretend it does not affect us. We sometimes run away from the pain but that keeps our hearts from healing and processing what has happened in a healthy way. There are times we must simply face the pain, feel it, and embrace it. Look to Jesus as our greatest example.

Jesus came to the tomb of his dead friend Lazarus. The family members had been waiting for Jesus to come heal him, but instead Lazarus died. "Therefore, when Jesus saw her [Mary] weeping, and the Jews who came with her weeping, He groaned in the spirit and was troubled. And He said, "Where have you laid him?" They said to Him, "Lord, come and see." Jesus wept. Then the Jews said, "See how He loved him" (John 11:33-35, NKJV)!

For two days after Hope's passing, I was unable to weep because I was in so much shock. It was as if I was in a bizarre twilight zone. But when we had to go back to our house to pick out her burial clothing, I finally broke down for the first time. As I cried, I heard another crying with me.

It was Jesus. Jesus was right there in my pain, weeping as I wept. He felt all of my pain with me.

In this passage of scripture, Jesus knew he could bring Lazarus back to life, but couldn't look past the suffering in front of him. He stood under the weight of pain, not as one who would suffer unto his coming death, but as one left to suffer with what an evil world would bring to the living.

The fall of man assured a broken world, one which would puncture the soul of everyone who journeys through it. Not one child of God would escape the tentacles of sin, sickness, and death because of man's free will. Jesus was feeling the grief, pain, and brokenness of this world.

While aware of the joy and life every believer would experience in eternity, Jesus was also fully engaged in the death, pain, and suffering life on earth would bring his children. The response of Jesus? He wept.

Jesus himself struggled with facing pain. In the garden before the soldiers took him away for crucifixion, Jesus felt the weight of all sin, sickness, and brokenness. He said, "Abba, Father, all things are possible for You. Take this cup away from Me; nevertheless, not what I will, but what You will" (Mark 14:36, NKJV). Jesus was so overwhelmed by pain and suffering, he asked for it to be removed. Do you see the process he had to go through in his own place of suffering? He wanted to run from enduring the pain, but shifted his focus to the mind of the Father. His response was to face the pain head on and allow God to use it. Did

God ever use it! Because of Jesus's willingness to endure pain, we are assured of our own victory over pain and suffering.

If you are under the weight of great pain today, Jesus longs to be there with you. He is willing to weep with you and experience your pain. He will give you power to overcome your place of suffering. It is okay to feel pain, to weep, to be undone, but do it in the presence of Jesus and suffer well in order to find hope.

Learn to Breathe

Have you ever felt so much pain that you could not even take a breath? It is almost as if someone hit you in the stomach and knocked the wind right out. Our response to that kind of pain can leave us in a panic, leading to anxiety attacks, fear, and even rage. It is as if you are deep under water, desperately doing everything you can to breathe again.

In the deepest moments of my own pain I learned how to breathe inside of Christ. I began to take very deep breaths and exhale slowly. Although I didn't realize it at the time, my reaction to pain was renewing life within me.

"And the Lord God formed man of the dust of the ground and breathed into his nostrils the breath of life; and man became a living being" (Genesis 2:7, NKJV). Mankind was just a lifeless, hopeless shell, until the Father breathed life into our nostrils. The moment God's breath hit Adam's internal being, the blood of our Father ran through his body, carrying life to every organ, bone, and muscle. Your blood does the same thing today. The moment the Father breathed his holy, perfect, loving breath into man, a union was created between his blood and ours. He joined our spirits together for eternity. When we receive Christ as our savior, we are reunited with him as a son or daughter. We become one and are made whole.

Take the time to invite Jesus into your place of suffering. Allow the spirit and the breath of God to heal you from the inside out. Imagine with each breath that Jesus is filling you with all of heaven. With every exhalation, the ugly painful blows of suffering are blown away. Learn to breathe in your pain with Jesus and the peace that passes all understanding will fill you up. His love will cast out all fear and Christ will victoriously erase all of your suffering.

Learn to Worship through the Pain

"At this, Job got up and tore his robe and shaved his head. Then he fell to the ground in worship and said: "Naked I came from my mother's womb, and naked I will depart. The LORD gave and the LORD has taken away; may the name of the LORD be praised" (Job 1:20-22).

I can't imagine anyone outside of Jesus who suffered more in life than Job. He lost all his children, everything he owned, and even his own health. Job didn't just pull up his bootstraps and carry on. He spent time facing his pain before the Lord. I imagine he spent many hours weeping before God and many moments trying to catch his breath as he felt one blow after another. But Job also worshipped the God who gave life and took it away in his place of suffering.

It took three months before I could even begin to sing or praise Jesus after my daughter's passing. I felt guilty and longed to feel his presence again. But every time I went into worship, I found myself longing to see Hope more. Then, a single encounter changed everything.

Our church was having a youth conference. We were familiar with the guest speaker and had sat under the ministry of this person for years with our children. Without our daughter Hope, the service felt painful. Being there was truly a sacrifice of worship. On this particular night, I heard the voice of the Lord ask of me, "Will you go and worship in the very spot your daughter was laid to rest?"

My heart jumped out of my chest just thinking about doing this. The church's altar was the place where Hope's lifeless body had laid in rest at her memorial service. Going to the altar and worshipping where she laid… This was a HUGE request of the Lord. Although I was afraid, after a time of hesitation I decided to go up. As I worshipped in that spot, my eyes caught one of the stickers our church had placed at the altar to identify "social distancing." During the pandemic, these areas were designated for people to stand. The spot read: "Hope Lives Here." It was a stark contradiction to her lifeless body that had been in that very place last January.

The more I worshipped, the more I felt the hope of the Lord and the life of my sweet girl. I heard the voice of the Lord: "Tonight you ordered hope into this room through your worship. I will break off the spirit of suicide upon my sons and daughters." And he did just that for many youth struggling with suicide that I knew personally. They received their healing that night. No one knew what the Father was speaking to me in those moments, but the youth minister followed the Lord's leading in ministry.

"And so, dear brothers and sisters, I plead with you to give your bodies to God because of all he has done for you. Let them be a living and holy sacrifice—the kind he will find acceptable. This is truly the way to worship him" (Romans 12:1, NLT). I want to encourage you to worship in your place of pain, sorrow, grief, anger, disappointment. There is nothing as pleasing to the Lord as the sacrifice of praise. He honors that worship and you will find hope within your reach. You will find joy, strength, and new perspective to help you through your trials. That night in worship, I found the goodness of the Lord as others were delivered. You will find His goodness too.

Learn to Never Give Up

We discussed this scripture earlier: "And not only that, but we also glory in tribulations, knowing that tribulation produces perseverance; and perseverance, character; and character, hope. Now hope does not disappoint, because the love of God has been poured out in our hearts by the Holy Spirit who was given to us" (Romans 5:3-5, NKJV).

Perseverance just means not quitting. Making up our mind that we will never quit is the very first thing we need to decide in order to suffer well in this world. My sweet Hope would be here today had she done this. I have had days where I felt like I could not go on anymore. I have had days where I felt like I would not be able to make it through the day. But quitting never became an option for me. I know what it is like to feel the pain of someone who has given up on life. The agony and suffering someone leaves behind after quitting is hell on earth. I could not do that to my family and loved ones. You must not give up either.

"The temptations in your life are no different from what others experience. And God is faithful. He will not allow the temptation to be more than you can stand. When you are tempted, he will show you a way out so that you can endure" (1 Corinthians 10:13, NLT). The meaning of the word temptation includes not just the temptation of sin, but temptation to give up and give in to your pain and suffering. You have lost your way and do not feel as if you can endure this world any longer. We all have been there. Our pain and suffering look different, but it always feels unbearable to go on. The key to the Lord's instructions is in this scripture. Invite Jesus into your hardest and deepest pain. When you want to just give up, he will show you a way of escape, and it will always be through him. If Jesus does not deliver you out of your circumstances, he will be everything you need in order to get through the situation. I am not able to have my daughter back on this earth again, but Jesus shows me how to walk through the pain, hour by hour. We cannot fix every circumstance, but Jesus can guide us through each one.

Our lives will always be filled with changes. A bad day, month or year will not stay that way forever. Life has mountains and valleys. There will be days of tremendous joy, deep sorrow, and even great anger. No season or situation remains the same indefinitely. My daughter failed to remember this truth in the moment. She could not see past her situation to the next day, much less five years down the road. Where you are right now, however you feel, and regardless of the situation you are currently going through, it will not be that way forever. Hope's choice to end her life that day was based upon lies she thought were true in one moment, of one day, in one situation. She responded impulsively to her emotions because she was unable to see beyond the rain. When you are in despair, set your mind, heart, and mouth to say, "I am not giving up!"

Learn to Find Joy

"This day is holy to our Lord. Do not grieve, for the joy of the Lord is your strength" (Nehemiah 8:10, NKJ).

This is a passage of scripture I have prayed for over two years now. It has not stopped me from grieving or feeling pain, for this is not what the Lord is saying. It is telling us: 'Do not be depressed or hopeless.' Then, the verse goes on to explain, "why." The Father's joy is our strength. Without godly joy, we become weak and without hope. Pain and suffering can rob us of all our strength. "A cheerful heart is good medicine, but a broken spirit saps a person's strength" (Proverbs 17:22, NLT). The Father has given us a remedy for our weakness and that is joy.

In my own place of pain, I started playing a daily game of "Hide and Seek" with the Lord to find joy. My days were by no means always full of joy, but I knew I could find a bit of joy each day for strength. One day it was in the rain that renewed the burning grass and plants in the heat of summer. Next it was the beauty of the rainbow following the rain, reminding my soul of God's promises. I found joy in the laughter of our youngest daughter filling our home. Joy was in the friendships of those gathered around our table who loved on us. I arose each day, like a child searching for candy, to find my joy. The purpose for each day became finding joy. As I looked day after day, my strength started to come back. Your joy might look different, but when you look for joy, you will find it. A few minutes of joy each day will help you find hope for the next day.

There is Hope

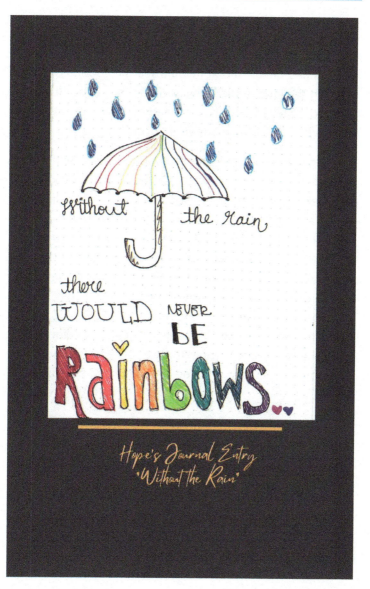

Hope's Journal Entry
"Without the Rain"

Learn to Find Purpose

A scripture worth repeating is: "I would have lost heart, unless I had believed that I would see the goodness of the LORD In the land of the living. Wait on the LORD; Be of good courage, and He shall strengthen your heart; Wait, I say, on the LORD!" (Psalms 27:13-1, NKJV).

The rain will stop. The Father's goodness will use all pain in your life to help you grow, to teach you, and to make you stronger. He will create a testimony in you that will help encourage and change someone else's life. As Jesus becomes your rainbow at the end of the storm, you will become the rainbow that points to the promise of the goodness of God for someone else. The most powerful people on this earth, who make the greatest difference, are those who have overcome tragedy and trials. Your trials and pain are going to make the beautiful color of Jesus shine brighter in your life. The Father's goodness is not subject to change. He does not have bad moods or bad days.

"You intended to harm me, but God intended it all for good. He brought me to this position so I could save the lives of many people" (Genesis 50:20, NLT). This scripture references Joseph, who was beaten and left to die by his own brothers. He was put in prison, but God used his life to save Israel from famine. Our enemy, Satan, is always out to harm us. He will use anyone and anything to destroy us. But God will use all his evil to create purpose in our lives.

There is Hope

I remember an evening sometime after Hope's passing. I was helping in our church's youth service. At the end of service, a young lady came up to the altar and I prayed for her. The next week she came back and searched for me to thank me for praying for her. The Father had done some remarkable things in her life that week after we prayed. She hugged me and I asked her what her name was so I could continue to pray for her. She said her name was HOPE! I was overcome by emotion. In that moment, I realized that God was going to use every bit of my pain to help a thousand girls just like my daughter. In that moment all the pain seemed to be washed away like a rainbow that appears after the rain. Jesus is the only one who can be the sun after a treacherous storm.

Your pain will not be in vain. God will use it if you learn to dwell in his midst. Learn, grow, and find a way for your testimony to help someone else. If we never experienced pain, how would we know the Father's strength, power, grace, mercy, and overcoming love? There is purpose in the pain. I promise you: The sun will rise, and your suffering will produce a rainbow!

There is Hope

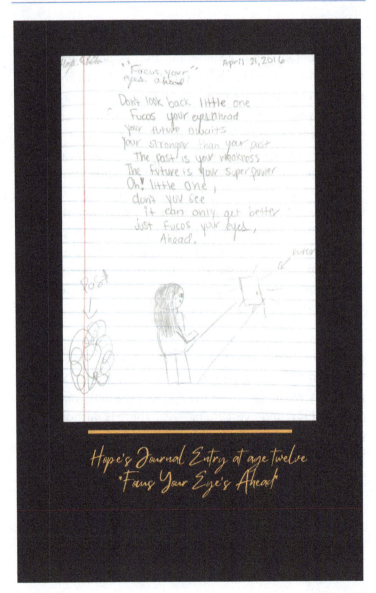

Hope's Journal Entry at age twelve
"Focus Your Eye's Ahead"

> "your not alone"
>
> Loneliness
> Fear
> Depression
> Anger
>
> All these things try to take you down
> it trys to sink you in a ship
> But your stronger than that
> your future is awaiting you
> your past is the past
> Don't worry about what's behind you,
> It's there for a reason.
> Deep inside you there is
> Courage
> happiness
> a loving soul
> all you have to do is reach in
> and have faith.
> your not alone.

Hope's Journal Entry at age twelve
"You Are Not Alone"

His Song Over You is Hope

There is Hope

The Father's song over you is HOPE:

Even in the worst of days and worst of circumstances

His will for you is good and not for evil

His goodness is the ONLY thing that will rescue you from the deepest pit of despair

I declare over you HOPE:

HOPE to breathe when it feels like you cannot anymore

HOPE to walk when it feels like you cannot even crawl

HOPE to hear what the Father is speaking louder over the lies of your enemy

HOPE to love and be loved

HOPE to laugh again

HOPE to find beauty in each day

HOPE to find purpose that goes beyond the hour or moment

HOPE to breathe deeply again

HOPE to cry

HOPE to laugh

HOPE to dream

HOPE to exhale

HOPE to stand

HOPE to wait

HOPE to see

HOPE that the Father will complete that which He began in you, now and throughout eternity. Find hope in Jesus.

Hope posted the following song to her Facebook page November 10, 2019, a few months before her passing. She quoted these words of the song that she thought were most powerful. She wrote:

"I thank God that His ink lasts longer than my words."

May the ink of God, His love and His truth, far outlast even the words of this book upon your heart.

Failure not worth it
It's too late to start again
And am sure am useless in the hands of the creator
Am not enough to salvage and am not enough to build with
So don't try
No I won't try
But then came your word healing a firming
Word write it on my heart write it on my mind
So I'll never forget it your word healing a firming word write it
On my heart write it on my mind so I'll never forget it your word
Walking around fearful what if someone finds out the
Truth that am shattered fixed together by the love of you
Not worthy of your attention am so guilty and ashamed
Please don't use me
No you can't use me
But here comes your word healing a firming word write it on my heart

There is Hope

Write it on my mind so I'll never forget it your word
healing write it on my heart write it
On my mind so I'll never forget it your word
Healing a firming word write it on my heart write it on my mind so
I'll never forget it your word healing a firming word write it
On my heart write it on my mind so I'll never forget it your word
I believe what you think about me
So I'll repeat the confession of your love for me
Now I breathe the life of your word in me
So I'll never forget it I believe what you think
About me so I'll repeat the confession of your love for me
Now I breathe the life of your word in me
So I'll never forget it
I believe what you think about me so I'll
Repeat the confession of your love for me
Now I breathe the life of your word in me
So I'll never forget it
I believe what you think about me
I'll repeat the confession of your love for
Me now I breathe the life of your word in me
So I'll never forget it
You know me completely
And yet you love me so deeply
Help me never forget it
And when mother and father forsake me
God you promise to take me up

Help me never forget it
Tonight we believe that we're purposed for you
Yes we are
God we're purposed by you
Help me never forget it
You love me so deeply
God your love is unchanging
God your love is unfailing
Help me never forget it

-Casey J, <u>Journal</u>

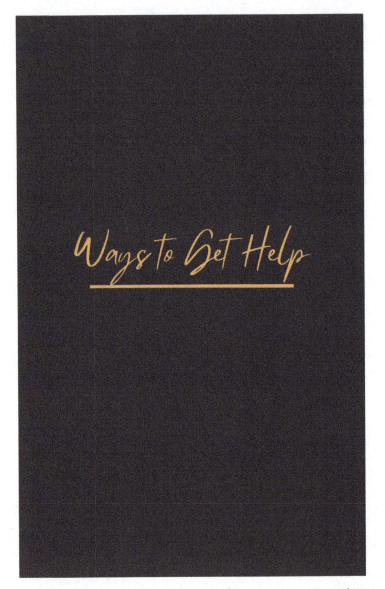

There is Hope

Please reach out for help if your emotions and thoughts are overwhelming and leading you to want to hurt yourself or others. First, if your parents are in your life and taking care of you, reach out to them. You may feel they will not understand, or they will feel disappointed in you, but I promise that is a lie Satan wants you to believe. Second, reach out to a trusted pastor or church leader. Third reach out to a counselor. Do one or all these things. There is never enough help.

National Suicide Prevention Lifeline

Hours: Available 24 hours. Languages: English, Spanish.

800-273-8255 website: suicidepreventionlifeline.org/

Your Life Your Voice-13 Reasons Why NOT

1-800-448-3000 Website: yourlifeyourvoice.org

Text to 20121: VOICE -for suicide hotline counselor

There is Hope

ONE WORD RESOLUTION

abide
John 15:4
John 15:7

BELIEVE
John 3:16
Romans 15:13
John 20:29

Content
Hebrew 13:5
Philippians 4:11-13
1 John 4:13

FEARLESS
Isaiah 41:10
2 Timothy 1:7
Joshua 1:9

Tongue
Ephesians 4:31-32
Leviticus 19:18
Colossians 3:13

GRATITUDE
Psalm 118:24
Psalms 136:1
Colossians 3:15

health
1 Corinthians 3:16
1 Corinthians 10:31
3 John 1:12

JOY
Proverbs 17:22
Philippians 4:4
Psalm 18:24

Love
1 Corinthians 13:13
Romans 13:9
1 Corinthians 13:4-7

MERCY
Luke 6:3
Matthew 5:7
Matthew 9:13

peace
1 Corinthians 14:33
Psalms 46:10
2 Thessalonians 3:16

TRUST
Psalm 28:7
Proverbs 3:5-6
Luke 1:37

Hope's Journal Entry
"Resolutions from Scripture"

There is Hope

Hope's Journal Entry
"Bible Verses for When You..."

Our story grabs the attention of every student we have the opportunity to share it with, and this open door has enabled us to be silence breakers, addressing

the weapons Satan has used in the dark halls of shame and guilt, especially within the body of Christ. Help starts with a cry. It is our mandate to initiate that cry for help through the power of the Holy Spirit and our testimony of tragedy and hope.

"Not only so, but we also glory in our sufferings, because we know that suffering produces perseverance; perseverance, character; and character, hope. And hope does not put us to shame, because God's love has been poured out into our hearts through the Holy Spirit, who has been given to us." Romans 5:3-5. Pain and suffering will affect everyone, and our youth and young adults are certainly not void of it, especially as the world continues to get dark. It is our heart to teach a generation how to suffer well that they might find hope at the end of their suffering.

Suffering well means to not just survive, but to thrive. It means to suffer in such a way that you become better and not bitter. In the midst of pain, you learn to find life, joy, and even purpose. You become an overcomer, because you learn to walk out your pain inside the one who overcame it all for you, Jesus. This generation has been coined "Hopeless and lonely", but where Satan has brought hopelessness, Jesus is bringing Hope and resurrection power!

Invite Us in to Speak at Your Church!

www.chosenstones.org

"I am so grateful that Kylie and I could attend last night. There aren't the right words to articulate all the emotions I felt leaving last evening. The anointing and presence of God was so powerful. Thank you from the bottom of my heart for being so vulnerable in sharing your loss and pain to reach so many in need. Hope's story and testimony is bringing life, restoration and healing to a generation in such need. Hell is losing its grip on our teens, and I believe many teens were set free last night. God Bless you always Alicia."

Made in the USA
Monee, IL
22 August 2025